THE AMAZING WORLD OF
PIRATES

DISCOVER THE EXCITING HISTORY OF PIRATICAL SAILORS AND BUCCANEERS

PHILIP STEELE

CONSULTANT: DAVID CORDINGLY

southwater

D0323277

This edition is published by Southwater, an imprint of Anness Publishing Ltd, Hermes House, 88–89 Blackfriars Road, London SE1 8HA tel. 020 7401 2077; fax 020 7633 9499

www.southwaterbooks.com; www.annesspublishing.com

If you like the images in this book and would like to investigate using them for publishing, promotions or advertising, please visit our website www.practicalpictures.com for more information.

UK agent: The Manning Partnership Ltd; tel. 01225 478444; fax 01225 478440; sales@manning-partnership.co.uk
UK distributor: Grantham Book Services Ltd; tel. 01476 541080; fax 01476 541061; orders@gbs.tbs-ltd.co.uk
North American agent/distributor: National Book Network; tel. 301 459 3366; fax 301 429 5746; www.nbnbooks.com
Australian agent/distributor: Pan Macmillan Australia; tel. 1300 135 113; fax 1300 135 103; customer.service@macmillan.com.au
New Zealand agent/distributor: David Bateman Ltd; tel. (09) 415 7664; fax (09) 415 8892

Publisher: Joanna Lorenz
Senior Editor: Gilly Cameron Cooper
Editorial Reader: Joy Wotton
Series Design: John Jamieson
Designer: Margaret Sadler
Illustration: Donato Spedaliere,
Colour Work: Clive Spong, Linden Artists
Picture Research: Charlotte Lippmann
Photography: John Freeman
Stylist: Melanie Williams

ETHICAL TRADING POLICY
Because of our ongoing ecological investment programme, you, as our customer, can have the pleasure and reassurance of knowing that a tree is being cultivated on your behalf to naturally replace the materials used to make the book you are holding. For further information about this scheme, go to www.annesspublishing.com/trees

PICTURE CREDITS
Ancient Art and Architecture Collection Ltd: 4cr, 5br, 10cr, 20br, 43bl, 50bl, 51tl, 55tr; Bridgeman Art Library: 16bl, 22bl, 23tr, 47b, 55br, 58br; English Heritage: 48b; The Art Archive: 5br, 9b, 29tl, 37t, 44bl; Mary Evans Picture Library: 8c, 10b, 14bl, 18bl, 25bl, 29cl, 30bl, 37br, 40br, 41tl, 41bl, 43tr, 51bl, 51br; Falmouth Museum: 12bl; The Fontomas Index: 11tr, 17br, 17bl, 28tr, 28cl, 36cr, 39tl, 57bl; Sonia Halliday Photographs: 46t; Robert Harding Picture Library: 13tr; Michael Holford Photographs: 8tr; Katz Pictures Ltd: 10tr, 41r; Museum of London: 43tl, 46c; National Maritime Museum: 9tr, 12tl, 17tr, 20c, 38bl, 39tr, 42t, 46br, 47tl, 51tr, 54t, 56br, 57cr; Peter Newark's Historical Pictures: 5t, 13tr, 16tl, 17tl, 24b, 25t, 25c, 25br, 36cl; Universitetets Oldsaksamling: 50tr; Parker Library, Corpus Christi College, Cambridge: 8b, 58c; Ann Ronan at Image Select: 4cl, 21tl, 21br, 42bl; York Archaeological Trust: 40tr. Peter Newark's Historical Pictures: front cover main picture

Previously published as Discovery: Pirates

☠ CONTENTS ☠

Death on the Horizon

Imagine a scene about 400 years ago. A Spanish treasure ship is homeward bound from the port of Cartagena in South America. It is loaded with chests of gold, silver and precious gems captured from the former Aztec empire. The wind is set fair. The sailor on lookout duty rubs his eyes. Is that a cloud on the horizon or a distant sail? Two hours later, the deck is soaked in blood and the ship is adrift and burning, a victim of piracy. The treasure will never reach the Spanish king.

Piracy means robbery at sea. It can still happen today, but until steam power replaced sail in the 1860s, ships were slow and heavy to manoeuvre, making them more vulnerable to attack. Many coasts were uncharted, and pirate ships could hide among remote creeks and islands, beyond the reach of the law. Piracy is as old as the history of shipping – the word itself comes from the ancient Greek word for attack. Pirates have also been called corsairs, buccaneers, freebooters, rovers, sea beggars and filibusters.

▲ DANGER AHEAD

A merchant seaman lookout watches a ship through his spyglass. There are suspiciously few crew on deck, and they are wearing an odd assortment of clothes. A bogus national flag has been replaced with the menacing skull and crossbones. It is a pirate ship.

▲ PIRATE OR HERO?

The English seafarer Francis Drake is knighted by Queen Elizabeth I in 1581. Drake had just returned from a voyage during which he raided Spanish colonies and shipping. His loot may have been £500,000 – about £70 million at today's values. To the English, Drake was a hero. To the Spanish, he was a common pirate. Many empire-building countries encouraged their seamen to attack ships of other nations.

CORSAIR ATTACK ▶

Dragut Rais was a corsair from the Barbary Coast of North Africa. The coast between Algiers and Tripoli was the scene of devastating Muslim attacks on ships from the Christian countries of the Mediterranean. Running warfare between the two faiths lasted from the 1500s to the 1800s. Dragut, a former slave of the Christians, became one of the greatest corsair commanders. He was killed at the Siege of Malta in 1565.

◀ THE CRUEL BUCCANEER

In the late 1660s, the Frenchman François l'Olonnois organized buccaneers (outlaws of the Caribbean) into pirate armies. At first the buccaneers had lived by hunting on Hispaniola and other islands, but they gradually turned to piracy. L'Olonnois was notorious for torturing his enemies. When he himself was taken prisoner by native warriors in Central America, his captors tore his body apart and burned it.

◀ **DEATH OF A PIRATE**
Edward Teach (otherwise known as Blackbeard) was the terror of North American waters until his violent death in 1718. His pirate ship *Adventure* was attacked by a British naval sloop under Lieutenant Robert Maynard. In a ferocious hand-to-hand battle in Ocracoke Inlet, North Carolina, Blackbeard was shot five times and received 20 sword wounds before he died. His head was hacked off and tied to the bowsprit of Maynard's ship, like a ghoulish figurehead.

◀ **PIRATES ON BOARD!**
An officer is at the pirates' mercy, and the crew is overpowered. The sailors might be given the choice of joining the pirates or being set adrift in a small boat. The pirates probably robbed any passengers, and then seized the whole ship, or just its supplies or the cargo.

A MODEL PRIVATEER ▶
Ships with a variety of different sails, like the model brig (*right*) and topsail schooners, were fast and manoeuvrable. This made them favourites with the pirates and privateers of the 1700s and 1800s. Privateers were captains who had been given legal authority to raid the merchant shipping of an enemy country. The ships of these official pirates were also called privateers. The line between privateering and piracy was often a very thin one.

Life at Sea

U ntil the 1800s no one gave much thought to conditions at sea for the common seaman, and life was hard for all sailors, pirates or not. Wooden ships of the 1600s and 1700s were cramped and uncomfortable. Pirate ships were often especially crowded because they had to take extra hands along to sail any captured vessels. The ships were unwieldy and pitched and tossed in the swell. Below deck, rats scampered in the darkness. The timbers creaked, and the bilges slopped in the depths of the ship. Lanterns shed a dim light, but open flames were forbidden, for fear that a spark would set off the gunpowder store. Bed was a lurching hammock or the corner of a storeroom. To go to the toilet, you had to squat over the head (a slatted box at the ship's bow with a hole open to the waves). Injury and disease were rife, and medical skills and supplies were minimal.

▲ GALLEY SLAVES

Corsair galley slaves are forced to row for their lives. They are whipped mercilessly and given barely enough food to stay alive. Along the Barbary Coast of Africa in the 1500s and 1600s, life was miserable whether you were a Christian slave on a Muslim corsair ship or a Muslim slave on a Christian corsair. In earlier times, oarsmen of the Greek pirate galleys also had a hard life, rowing on hard benches and exposed to the burning sun, but at least they were free.

PUTTING ASHORE ▶

A ship's company goes ashore on a coral island to re-stock. Storage casks were filled with fresh water, and on tropical islands, there were coconuts and fresh fruit to pick. The crew could fish, and hunt seabirds, wild animals and giant turtles for fresh meat. When Captain Kidd's crew landed on the Laccadives (modern Lakshadweep) off the coast of India in the late 1600s, they also plundered and terrorized local villages.

◀ BAD COMPANY

Pirates drank and gambled to break the boredom of a long voyage. Most were rough seamen, and many had long lived on the wrong side of the law. Fights were common. In 1697, the Scottish privateer Captain William Kidd killed one of his own crew, gunner William Moore, by smashing him over the head with a bucket. About 20 years later, Blackbeard shot his ship's master, Israel Hands, through the knee. Frayed tempers were a particular problem when a ship was becalmed for days through lack of wind.

◀ **DISHING IT UP**

The ship's cook creates another disgusting meal. On a long voyage, most food had to be preserved by salting and drying, although hens might be kept on board for fresh eggs and meat. Biscuits called hard tack were often riddled with weevils (insects). Chinese pirates are on record as eating the ship's rats. Lack of vitamin C from fresh fruit and vegetables in the diet led to a horrible disease called scurvy.

▲ **SLUNG BETWEEN THE CANNON**

A ship's crew starts a drinking bout on the gundeck. Heavy cannon were rolled back from the gunports and secured with ropes. Tables were slung from the beams, so that they could easily be stowed away during battle. Cloth hammocks, a South American invention, could also be cleared away quickly. They were used on British ships from 1597.

▲ **SCRUBBING THE DECKS**

A group of regular sailors is ordered to scrub the deck. Pirates were used to scenes like this on naval and merchant ships they had sailed on. The jobs still had to be done on pirate ships to keep the vessel seaworthy, but crews shared the work. They agreed a set of rules to cover aspects of everyday life such as care of fighting equipment and sharing of prizes from victims' ships. They could even elect to overthrow the captain.

▲ **ALL IN A DAY'S WORK**

Days at sea were an almost endless round of hard labour. Cannon were cleaned and kept in good running order. Heavy sails were raised and furled with changes in wind speed and direction, spars and masts repaired after battles or storms, frayed ropes spliced and joined. The pirates worked in watches (four-hour shifts), taking it in turns to sail the ship and to be on the lookout for land – and their next victim.

A Pirate Ship

A ship like the one in this picture outpaced and outmanoeuvred the heavier warships of its day. It is very like the *Adventure Galley*, which was built in 1695 for Scottish-born Captain William Kidd, a privateer and businessman who lived in New York City. Kidd's official mission was to hunt other pirates, but he ended up being accused of piracy himself. The *Adventure Galley* weighed 281 tonnes and was 38m long – bigger than many pirate vessels of the time. It was built in Deptford near London, England, and sailed to New York in April 1696 with a crew of 70. The following September, it left with a crew of 152, bound for the Indian Ocean. Under full sail, Kidd's ship could reach speeds of up to 14 knots (27km/hour). When the wind failed, it could be operated by the long oars, called sweeps. Although the ship was new, it leaked badly and was abandoned by Kidd in Madagascar, where it was stripped of valuables and burnt.

KEY

1 bowsprit	11 fore staysail	22 gundeck
2 mainsail	12 stern lantern	23 sweeps
3 spritsail	13 mizzen	24 bilges
4 topgallants	14 foremast	25 pumps
5 mizzen mast	15 gunwale	26 water casks
6 ratlines	16 foresail	27 gunport
7 yards	17 sail locker	28 anchor
8 jib	18 topsails	
9 foc's'le	19 magazine	
10 quarterdeck	20 crow's nest	
	21 shot locker	

▲ **COOK'S AREA**

A kitchen on board ship is called a galley – a word that is also used for a large ship with oars. This one was in the fo'c'sle (the raised deck at the front of the ship). A bucket of sand stood by the stove to put out fires. Pirates often died from scurvy and cholera because of the poor diet.

◄ THE GUNDECK
Each of the *Adventure Galley's* 34 guns fired cannonballs that weighed 5.4kg each. This made it capable of taking on most merchant ships of the day. The ship carried 1,000 spare cannonballs in a locker in the hold and plenty of gunpowder in the magazine.

▲ THE CAPTAIN'S CABIN
The most comfortable part of the ship was the grand cabin at the stern. This was where the captain plotted the course of his voyage, gave orders to the crew and ate his meals. Here were his navigating instruments and his personal weapons, ready to hand in case of mutiny or sudden attack.

▲ THE CAPSTAN
The anchor was so heavy that it needed to be raised by a winding gear called a capstan. Bars were slotted into the top, so that it could be pushed round and round. It was backbreaking work, often done to the accompaniment of singing or fiddle music.

A Speedy Sloop

The word sloop was first used in 1629 to describe a small and nippy sailing ship suited to sailing coastal waters rather than great oceans. A typical sloop of those days had a long, standing bowsprit to support the small foresails. These small sails made the ship more manoeuvrable. A sloop usually had one mast, which carried the mainsail. The boats were used by Caribbean pirates because their shallow draught (depth under water) made them easy to beach in hidden creeks and lagoons. The pirate haunts of Bermuda and Jamaica became famous for building fine sloops in the 1700s.

1 Copy templates **A**, **B**, **C** and **H** on to dark brown card, and **D** on to light card. Copy the sail templates **E**, **F**, and **G** on to the fabric. Pierce the mark for the mast hole on the deck section **D** with the knitting needle.

You will need: *one A2 sheet of dark brown card, one A3 sheet of light brown card, 40cm² cream cotton fabric, pencil, ruler, knitting needle, scissors, strong paper glue, adhesive tape, acrylic paints, paintbrush, cold stewed tea, 1.5m balsa wood dowel, 2.4cm diameter, cut into five pieces 12cm, 22cm, 13cm, 24cm and 50cm long, strong black sewing thread, strong darning needle.*

5 Glue one side of the keel and rudder section **C**, leaving the edges unglued. Fold the section in half and pinch the glued areas so that they stick together.

6 Now put glue on the unglued edges. These stick on either side of the hull when you fit the keel and rudder section **C** into position.

7 Bend the tabs on the deck section **D** downwards. Put glue on the outside of each tab. Ease the deck section **D** into the top of the boat's hull.

10 Oversew the top of the mainsail **E** to the 12cm dowel and the bottom to the 22cm dowel. Sew around the dowel and through the sail.

11 Glue the 13cm dowel about 6cm from the top of the 50cm dowel (mast) to make a long cross shape. This cross spar supports the tops of the sails.

12 Push the needle through the tops of the foresails **E** and **G** and the spar, then knot the thread. Join the bottom, pointed corners to the 24cm dowel.

13 Use the knitting needle to make an indent on the other side of the mast about 14cm up. Fill with glue. Insert the 22cm mainsail dowel.

12cm

D
DECK

25cm

6cm

Cut out all templates apart from the sails (**E**, **F** and **G**).

2 Cut 2½cm slits at the three points marked with a dotted line on hull section **A**. Overlap these to make the hull's curved shape. Glue them into position.

3 Cut three slits in exactly the same way on the second hull section **B**. This time, overlap them in the opposite direction. Glue the overlapping pieces into place.

4 Join the two hull sections **A** and **B** together on the inside with adhesive tape. Fold over the stern section to fit into the hull. Glue the tabs inside the hull.

8 Paint thin brown lines along the length of the deck for planks. Paint a pale stripe along the top of the hull with gun holes and portholes.

9 Draw vertical lines on to the sails. Cut out the sails with scissors. If you like, you can stain them by brushing with stewed tea.

14 When the glue is dry, attach the mainsail **E** top. Take the thread around the dowel at the top of the sail. Push it through the spar and knot.

15 Glue the foot of the mast into the masthole. Glue bowsprit holder **H** in front of the mast. Fit the dowel holding the foresails into it.

Real sloops were built for trading, privateering and also for naval anti-piracy patrols. Your boat is neither seaworthy nor waterproof, so do not try sailing it in the bath.

Attack at Sea

In port, pirate spies would try to find out which ships had the richest cargoes, and when and where they were sailing. Pirates might trail their prey for days, keeping just out of sight – for the key to any successful attack was surprise. They might pose as a harmless merchant vessel, or lurk behind a headland and then suddenly sail out to confront their victims. Sometimes the most successful pirate actions were so foolhardy, that the enemy was simply dumbfounded. In the 1700s, the flamboyant pirate captain Bartholomew Roberts would cause panic by sailing into the thick of an enemy fleet, even though he was hopelessly outnumbered, but with drums beating and all guns blazing.

As soon as the target ship came within range – of catapults or bows and arrows in ancient times, or cannon from the 1400s onwards – serious shooting would begin. When the victim's ship was disabled, the pirates would prepare to board. The fate of the ship was then decided by hand-to-hand combat.

▲ **BOARDING PARTY**
The towering stern of a Spanish treasure ship looms above an attacking pirate crew. Their small boarding vessel is out of the galleon's firing line and so easy to control that the pirates can quickly come up alongside, ready to board.

▲ **HOLDING FAST!**
A pirate of the 1700s hurls a grappling iron over to the enemy ship. The iron's anchor-like hooks would take hold in the shrouds (ropes), so that the ship could be hauled close to. Pirates terrified their victims before boarding by cursing and yelling bloodthirsty threats. Fear was probably their most effective weapon.

◄ **BATTERING RAMS**
Pointed, metal-plated rams were fitted on the prows of ancient Greek and Roman galleys. They were designed to smash through the hull of an enemy ship. The galley would be rowed at maximum speed (perhaps 15km/hour) straight towards the enemy. Sailors from the Greek island of Rhodes devised some very crafty tricks. They used their oars to make the prow dip just before the point of collision, so that the ram holed the enemy ship as deeply as possible below the waterline.

◄ **FINAL STAGE**
A Turkish crew battles with Greek corsairs during the 1800s. Once two ships had closed with each other, a sea attack became more like a traditional land battle, with the ships serving as floating platforms for hand-to-hand combat. Turkish fleets often carried units of crack troops called janissaries.

◄ CALM WATERS
Barbary galleys go into action against Venetian ships off the port of Patras in Greece, in 1751. From the Middle Ages onwards, Venice was one of the richest trading ports in Italy. Its shipping was regularly attacked by Uskok pirates (from what is now Croatia) and by Barbary corsairs from North Africa. Barbary galleys rarely travelled far from their home ports. They were designed for attack in the relatively calm Mediterranean rather than for the open ocean.

▲ PIRATES IN BONNETS
Pirates prepare to board an American vessel, going to great lengths to deceive their victims as to their true identity. Some of them crouch out of sight, armed to the teeth. Others are disguised as female passengers parading for the benefit of the American captain's telescope. Surprise is an essential weapon for a successful attack.

CHINESE TACTICS ►
Chinese pirates board a ship from a simple rowing boat lowered from their main junk. Some of these small boats were armed with light guns and could carry up to 20 heavily armed pirates. Such attacks were still common in the South China Sea in the early 1900s. They became less effective when Dutch and English steam-powered gunboats were introduced to the area.

Fancy Figurehead

Decorative prows and figureheads have been put on ships since ancient times. Many were designed to bring good luck to the ship or to keep evil at bay. The prows of the galleys used by pirates and pirate hunters in ancient Rome often rose into a great curve that was ornately carved and painted or gilded. Some ancient Mediterranean galleys were decorated with big eyes (to ward off evil), victory wreaths, animals or figures. The prows of Viking longships were often carved into snarling dragon heads, which must have looked terrifying as a raiding party emerged from a ghostly sea mist.

You will need: *60 x 30cm corrugated cardboard, pencil, ruler, scissors, a lot of old newspapers, masking tape, cup of flour, about ½ cup of water, bowl, fork, fine sandpaper, red, white and black acrylic paints, thick paintbrush, white card, craft knife, glue, thin paintbrush.*

1 Following the measurements shown above, copy the basic figurehead shape on to the large piece of corrugated cardboard.

Ajax, legendary hero of the Trojan Wars in ancient Greece, is the model for this splendid figurehead. He stood at the head of a 74-gun ship of the 1800s. Most naval patrol ships and some of the larger vessels captured as pirates' prizes had splendid figureheads. However, smaller, workaday pirate vessels were rarely so fancy.

4 Cover the whole base with a layer of paper balls. Add extra layers to the chest and face. Add an extra, fist-sized piece for the nose. Leave space for the eyes.

5 Twist the newspaper into sausages for jaw, lips and brows. Make two thick pieces for the paws (see Step **10** for shape). Tape everything into place.

8 Make two table tennis ball-sized eyes from paste and newspaper. Leave everything in a warm place until dry and hard. Smooth with sandpaper.

9 Use the thick brush to paint the front and back of the figurehead in a bright colour. This figure is red, but rich yellow or blue would be good too.

10 Cut white card triangles for claws and teeth. Make slits in the paws and mouth with a craft knife, then glue teeth and claws into them.

2 Carefully cut out all round the figurehead shape. It will be easier if you do a section at a time, as shown above, and you will not bend the board.

3 Scrunch up sheets of newspaper into tight balls. Place each ball on top of the cardboard cutout. Tape them on with the masking tape.

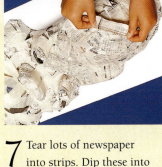

6 Put the flour into the bowl, and, mixing all the time with a fork, gradually add water. The paste should be thick and smooth like pancake batter.

7 Tear lots of newspaper into strips. Dip these into the paste and cover the front and back of the figure with three layers of strips.

11 Paint the eyeballs white. When the paint is dry, add a black dot for the pupils. Glue the eyeballs on. Paint on the eyebrows and nostrils.

12 Use the fine paintbrush and the black paint to paint in other decorative details such as the fur.

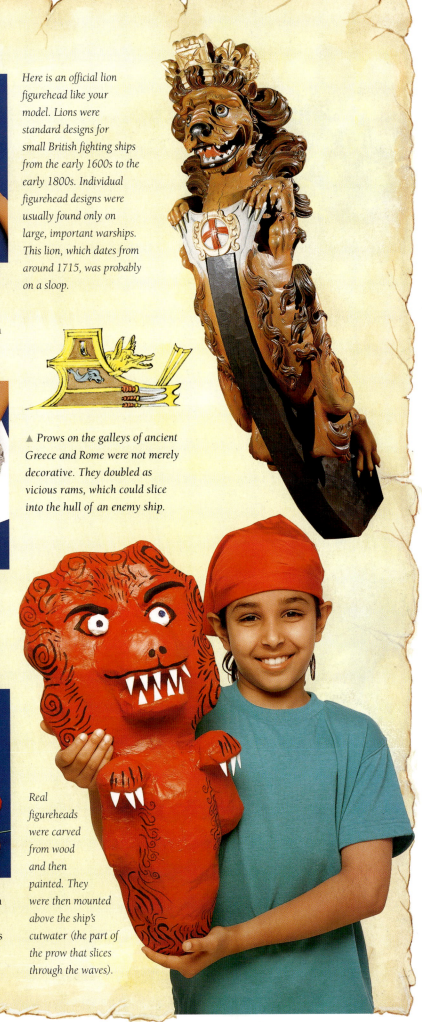

Here is an official lion figurehead like your model. Lions were standard designs for small British fighting ships from the early 1600s to the early 1800s. Individual figurehead designs were usually found only on large, important warships. This lion, which dates from around 1715, was probably on a sloop.

▲ *Prows on the galleys of ancient Greece and Rome were not merely decorative. They doubled as vicious rams, which could slice into the hull of an enemy ship.*

Real figureheads were carved from wood and then painted. They were then mounted above the ship's cutwater (the part of the prow that slices through the waves).

Coastal Raids

Ships were never the only target for pirates. They raided coastal settlements in search of treasure, food or villagers they could sell as slaves. The Vikings were even prepared to join forces with rival crews, sail up rivers far inland, and attack whole cities. They besieged Paris in AD885 and pulled down London Bridge in 1009.

In 1627 the inhabitants of Reykjavik in Iceland were astounded to be raided, plundered and enslaved by Barbary corsairs from North Africa. This fleet was led by Dutchman Jan Jansz, who called himself Murad Rais. He was one of many European seafarers who turned Turk (joined the other side) and fought for the Muslim Barbary corsairs. It was these renegades who, for a time, persuaded the North Africans to break with custom and sail further afield.

Pirate trickery worked just as well on land as at sea. In 1719 the Welsh pirate Howell Davis managed to convince the commander of a Royal Africa Company fort in Gambia that he was a legitimate trader from Liverpool. Davis overpowered his host during dinner, and sailed off with gold bars and ivory from the company store.

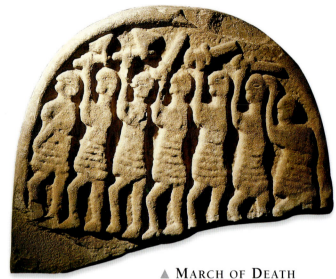

▲ **MARCH OF DEATH**
A bloodthirsty crew of Vikings is carved on a gravestone. The warriors are armed with swords and battle axes. The carving may record the events of June AD793, when Viking pirates descended on the little island of Lindisfarne, off the north-east coast of England. They plundered the monastery, murdered the monks and then set fire to the buildings.

▲ **LAND HUNGRY**
Viking pirates from Scandinavia scan the coastline, searching out weak points in the defences. They will run their longships ashore, and attack with axes, spears, swords and burning arrows. Green hills were particularly appealing to Vikings in search of good land where they could settle. Much of their homeland in Scandinavia was poor heathland, barren mountain or snowy forest.

◄ **CATTLE RAIDERS**
A buccaneer rounds up stolen cattle during a raid on Santo Domingo on the island of Hispaniola. Raiders would sell cattle meat and hides to passing ships and make a useful profit. The cattle owners often suffered more than the loss of their animals. Many were tortured and killed by the buccaneers. Today, Hispaniola is occupied by the Dominican Republic and Haiti. During the 1500s and most of the 1600s, it was all ruled by Spain and under constant attack. From the 1630s, the west of the island became a base for the buccaneers.

◄ SPANISH-HELD TREASURE
An evil-looking bunch of buccaneers sacks the port of Cartagena, the largest Spanish city on the Caribbean coast of South America. In the 1630s, a steady stream of mule trains carried silver from the mines of Peru to be shipped back to Spain. Some Spanish towns were held to ransom by privateers and buccaneers time and time again.

▲ BUCCANEER ARMY RAID
In 1668, Henry Morgan led an army of English and French buccaneers into the Cuban town of Puerto del Principe (modern Camaguey). Over 700 heavily armed buccaneers marched inland, fighting their way mercilessly into the Spanish-ruled town. They killed a hunded soldiers and took many hostages. Local people were locked in churches while the buccaneers stole valuables from their homes. This was the first of Morgan's brutal, but very effective raids.

◄ HUMAN CARGO
A pirate crew seizes slaves from West Africa. Throughout history, slave trading and piracy went hand in hand. In the 1600s and 1700s, pirates could make a very large profit selling slaves to the new colonies in the Americas, at 10 to 15 times what they had paid for them. The pirates bartered with tribal chiefs, exchanging cheap gifts or currency for the slaves. Sometimes they kidnapped the slaves themselves.

Hand Weapons

According to the ship's rules drawn up by pirate Captain George Lowther in the 1720s, the first crew member to spot a sail on the horizon would be rewarded with the best pistol on that ship, if it was captured. Personal weapons were the tools of a pirate's trade, and captured weapons were highly valued prizes. Pirates cared for their arms, cleaning them regularly and keeping them dry, for their lives depended on the weapons being in good working order.

Over the ages, a pirate's personal arms included every type of weapon imaginable – clubs, spears, daggers, swords, pistols and muskets. Some weapons became particularly associated with pirates. The Vikings are remembered for their battle axes. The swords of the Barbary corsairs were of the highest quality steel and finely crafted. The buccaneers of the Caribbean were famed as sharpshooters (experts with the musket and the flintlock pistol). Pirates of south-east Asia used spears, darts from blowpipes and very ornate swords – some of the handles were decorated with human hair. The most common and useful pirate weapon was probably the cutlass, a sword used by pirates and other sailors from the 1600s onwards.

◄ **BUTCHER'S KNIFE**

The simple but deadly cutlass may have its origins in the long knives used by the first buccaneers to butcher their cattle. A guard protects the hand and the blade is short and broad compared with a sword. Cutlasses, pikes and axes were used by the ship's company, while a pirate captain or naval officers might carry more elaborate swords.

▲ **STRAIGHT TO THE POINT**

A bold thrust of the cutlass at the throat of a senior officer, and the battle is as good as won. The sturdy cutlass was the standard weapon for close fighting until the late 1800s. It was less likely than a rapier to be caught in the ropes and sails on board ship.

◄ **MAD MUSKETEERS**

Wielding a musket was not easy, especially on an unsteady deck. A long rod was needed to reload, and the muzzle rested on a special support (the musket rest) ready for firing. Nevertheless, rust-proof muskets decorated with brass were specially designed for use at sea in the late 1600s. The weapons were also used by buccaneer armies of the 1600s when they raided the cities of the Spanish Main. Effective firing range was about 100m. A spark from a flint ignited the gunpowder charge and fired the lead musket ball.

1700s

1743

1740-45

1740-45

◀ ONE SHOT
Flintlock pistols
aimed to stop an
attacker dead at short
range. They were
used for fighting
on board from the 1730s
to the 1830s. Pulling the
trigger made a flint strike a
metal plate and cause a
spark. This fired the
gunpowder. Flintlocks fired
a single lead ball and a pistol was often carried
in each hand so that two shots were possible.

▲ CHINESE DAGGERS
European passengers panic as
Chinese pirates board a
French steamship in the
1900s. Chinese pirates fought
with firearms, bamboo spears,
lethal-edged pikes and short
swords with hooked blades.
Victims were often beheaded.
Piracy continued in the South
China Sea until the 1920s.

◀ FIGHTING AT
CLOSE QUARTERS
A naval crew boards a Barbary
corsair, with cutlasses drawn.
At close quarters, these short
slashing swords were much
more effective than long
stabbing swords, such as
rapiers. One sailor uses his
pistol butt as a club. This
particular battle was in 1816
when a combined British and
Dutch naval fleet attacked the
North African port of Algiers.

Cut-throat Cutlass

The swords carried by pirates varied greatly over the ages. Ancient Greek pirates might fight with a leaf-shaped blade about 60cm long or with a curved cut-and-thrust blade called a *kopis*. Their Roman enemies fought with a short sword called the *gladius*. Viking swords were long and double-edged, for heavy slashing. The rapier, introduced in the 1500s, was a very light sword with a deadly, pointed blade, but was too long and delicate for close-range fighting on board ship. The cutlass was the ideal weapon for that. The best quality steel was made by the Arabs, and would have used by Barbary corsairs.

1 Lay one piece of the stiff card on a flat surface. Use a pencil to outline carefully the shape of the cutlass blade and hilt on to the cardboard.

2 Cut out the shape and use this as a template to lay on the second piece of card. Draw around the template and then cut out a second cutlass shape.

You will need: 2 pieces of stiff card 45 x 5cm, pencil, scissors, glue, newspaper, masking tape, 1 piece stiff card 30 x 10cm, 1 cup of flour, about ½ cup of water, mixing bowl, fork, fine sandpaper, brown and silver acrylic paint, two 2.5cm paintbrushes, black felt-tipped pen, ruler, wood varnish.

5 Take the third piece of card measuring 30 x 10cm. Draw the cutlass handle shape to fill the whole length of the card. Carefully cut it out.

6 Hold the narrow stem of the handle in one hand and scissors in the other. Cut down the middle of the wide end to about 2.5cm short of the stem.

7 Tape the narrow stem of the handle to the end of the cutlass hilt. Bend the rest of the handle round to slot over the curved edge of the blade.

The characters of Blackbeard the Pirate and Abdulla the Prince fight with cutlasses in this toy theatre production of the 1800s. The excitement and drama of a sword fight became a popular feature of many swashbuckling plays, pantomimes and, later, films about pirates.

12 Paint the cutlass blade and handle with two coats of acrylic paint. Allow each coat of paint to dry thoroughly before you apply the next.

3 Lay the two matching sections on top of each other. Glue them together. The double thickness gives the finished cutlass extra strength.

Cutlasses were still being used 200 years after they were first introduced. In this vicious clash of 1809, Lieutenant John Turner and his British crew were overwhelmed by a Chinese pirate crew. The rivers and islands around the major international port of Canton (Guangzhou) were thick with pirates. The Europeans called them Ladrones, from the Portuguese word for robbers.

4 Twist newspaper into thick strips to wind around the hilt. This should be enough to make a thick handgrip. Bind the newspaper with masking tape.

8 Make sure the oval lies flat against the hilt (to form a hand guard). Use masking tape to seal the slit and to secure the handle to the blade.

9 Put the flour in a bowl and slowly add water, a spoon at a time, mixing as you go. The paste should be smooth and thick like pancake batter.

10 Tear newspaper into short strips, coat these with paste and cover the whole of the cutlass three layers thick.

11 Leave the cutlass in a warm place for several hours. When completely hard and dry, smooth with sandpaper.

13 Leave the background paint surface to dry completely. Then use the black pen and a ruler to draw details on the blade, as shown above.

14 Finally, use a clean brush to apply a coat of wood varnish. This will toughen the cutlass as well as giving it a menacing glint.

The true cutlasses used by pirates and sailors from the 1600s onwards would have had a steel blade and a brass or iron hilt (handle). To stop the blade rusting – a problem you will not have with yours – the pirates would have rubbed grease on the blade.

Fire and Smoke

The aim of a pirate attack was to disable a ship, not to destroy it, and so make sure there was something left to steal. In ancient times, this was often achieved by firing flaming arrows into the rigging of enemy ships.

Gunpowder (a mixture of saltpetre, sulphur and charcoal) was invented in China in the AD800s. The Arabs knew of gunpowder by the 1200s and called it Chinese snow. However, it could not be effectively used as ammunition until bronze or iron barrels strong enough to contain the explosive force were made in the 1300s. Cannon became a standard fitting on fighting ships from the early 1500s, but accidents were common. Gunpowder was dangerous stuff, especially when handled by drunken or careless crews. Some buccaneers even tried mixing it with their rum and drinking it! In 1669 the magazine (the place where the gunpowder was stored) blew up on the Welsh pirate Henry Morgan's ship, the *Oxford*. Over 200 buccaneers were killed.

Pirates of the 1700s were expert at making hand grenades (wooden or iron pots filled with explosives). They also packed boats with gunpowder, set a fuse and let them drift into the enemy fleet. These boats were known as *brûlots* (fireships).

▲ GREEK FIRE

The notorious pirate fleets of the Mediterranean had access to a fearful new weapon between AD671 and 900. It was called Greek fire, an explosive cocktail of sulphur, quicklime and an inflammable spirit like petroleum, called naphtha. Jets of burning liquid were sprayed over the enemy from flamethrowers mounted on board ship and caused the most terrible injuries. Despite its name, Greek fire was probably first used in Byzantium (modern Istanbul).

▲ ROUND SHOT

Cannon and musket balls like these were solid lumps of iron hurled at deadly speed from the muzzle of the gun. The ammunition expelled from a cannon or a musket by an explosion of gunpowder was called shot. Sometimes a lethal mixture of small iron pieces called grapeshot was fired from cannon too.

END OF AN ERA ▶

The Dutch and English join forces in a fiery end to the centuries-long reign of the Barbary pirates. Following this dramatic 1816 sea battle off the corsair stronghold of Algiers, more than 1,000 Christian slaves were freed. It was announced that piracy was at an end, and many corsair galleys were scrapped or burned.

▲ LAND ATTACK

Fire from cannon and muskets blasts
the field of battle as the Dutch under
Pieter van der Deks plunder the
Canary Islands in 1599. Ships' crews
carrying out raids on coastal positions
had to be very skilled. Cannons on
land were heavier and more powerful
than those on ships. Although at this
time sea cannons on Spanish galleons
had a range of about 400m, most
pirate ship cannons would have not
have been able to fire that far.

AVERY'S CANNON ▶

The British pirate Henry Avery poses
at the scene of his most impressive
victory. He fought against the
Moghul fleet off Bombay in 1695 and
captured two ships. His ship, the
Fancy, carried 46 guns, but the
Moghul treasure ship *Gang-i-sawai*
shown in the picture, had 62. Avery's
gunners aimed to bring down the
masts, spars and sails of their victims'
ships rather than sink them.

◀ EASTERN GUNFIRE

In 1843 the British naval vessel HMS
Dido patrolled the North Borneo coast
on behalf of James Brooke, who was
the British ruler of Sarawak. In the
mid-1800s, European interest in
south-east Asia led to an increase in
trade and shipping. This meant rich
pickings for the local pirates, who were
known as dayaks. The British quest
was to destroy the pirate bases and
fleets of galleys called prahus. The
naval crews transferred to prahus so
that they could sail up the shallow
rivers. South-east Asian pirates defended
themselves with swivel guns (small
mounted cannon), but these were not
very effective when pitted against
superior European fire power.

Cannon at the Ready

In battle, the ships would manoeuvre to bring the enemy within their field of fire. Firing each cannon was a skilled but exhausting and dangerous task that could keep half-a-dozen men busy. The gun was run in and out of the gunport on a wheeled mounting, and was tightly secured by ropes. These secured the gun when it recoiled from the shot, flying backwards. Iron cannons were used in Europe by the 1300s, and the Europeans soon overtook the Chinese in the development of firearms. By the 1500s, even pirates were master gunners, and their ships were large enough to carry cannon.

1 Copy the templates, following the measurements shown above. Use thick card for all of them apart from the wheel and wheel rim templates, which should be on thin card. Cut all the templates out.

You will need: 30 x 30cm piece of stiff card, 15 x 15cm piece of thin card, pencil, ruler, scissors, wood glue, thick and thin paintbrushes, red and black paint, pair of compasses, 12.5 x 2cm strip of corrugated card, masking tape, 2 cardboard tubes about 13cm long, one 4cm diameter, one 3cm diameter, self-hardening clay, knitting needle or bradawl, 9cm length of ½cm-diameter dowel, kebab stick.

6 Take the thinner of the two cardboard tubes. Wrap the 12.5 x 5cm strip of corrugated cardboard around one end. Secure with masking tape.

7 Glue the outer edge of the corrugated card ring. Insert the thinner cardboard tube into the wider cardboard tube to make the muzzle of the cannon.

8 Cover the join between the inner and outer tubes by gluing on a strip of clay. Glue a thin roll of clay to the rim of the cannon's mouth and leave to dry.

On board ship, cannon were often mounted on wheeled carriages, like this 32-pounder of the 1700s. The gunpowder was rammed down the barrel of the cannon. The more firmly it was packed, the more effective the explosion. A smouldering fuse set off the gunpowder charge with an almighty crash, and the shot hurtled toward its target. If the cannon balls burst into the hull or decks of a wooden ship, the impact caused a lethal shower of giant splinters. More deaths were caused by splinters than by the shot itself.

11 Pierce holes through the centre of each wheel with the knitting needle or bradawl. Be careful not to break them as they are quite delicate.

2 Glue the two sides **D** to **B**. Add end pieces **A** and **C**. Push **G** inside so it's slightly lower than the semi-circles on **D**. Let each section dry before adding the next.

3 Use the thick paintbrush to paint the cannon base in one or two coats of bright red acrylic paint. Let the first coat dry before you apply the second.

4 Use a pair of compasses to draw the 4.5cm-diameter wheel sections on the thin card. Draw four wheel sections altogether, then cut them out.

5 Glue the two strips of card **E** around two of the circles. Glue the other two circles on top of the rim to make the drum-like wheels. Paint the wheels black.

9 Make two holes through the narrow barrel with the bradawl. Enlarge them with the handle of a paintbrush. Insert the dowel and glue in place.

10 Use the thick paintbrush to paint the cannon and dowel with black paint. Allow the first coat to dry before applying a second coat.

A real cannon is described by the weight of the shot it can fire. The biggest guns on the largest naval warships of the 1700s were 32-pounders (23kg). Most guns on a pirate ship would be much smaller. Remember that your cannon is not made of metal. It will make an impressive display item in your room, but you should not try to fire it or play with matches.

12 Pierce the cannon base towards the front end with the kebab stick. Feed the stick through both holes. Put the wheels on the stick as shown.

13 Cut the kebab stick to the right length, leaving ¾cm poking out beyond the wheels. Put a blob of clay on the ends to keep the wheels in place.

Pirate Treasure

Like any modern robbers, pirates throughout history wanted to win treasure that was valuable, easily transported and readily sold. Gold, silver and precious stones were always their first choice, either in the form of coins, ingots, jewellery, tableware or crosses stolen from churches. Vikings would even steal church bells and melt down the metal. Fine quality cloths, such as silks and heavy embroidered materials were always worth taking, and so was ivory. Sam Bellamy's *Whydah*, wrecked in a storm off Cape Cod, Massachusetts, in 1717, was discovered in 1983. The ship carried pieces-of-eight, gold bars and West African jewellery.

Many pirates' prizes were not at all glamorous, such as saltfish, hides, rare dyes, tobacco, spices or loaves (solid blocks) of sugar. Bulk cargoes were sometimes unwelcome because they were difficult to unload and sell without attracting attention. Equipment and supplies were always in demand, and captured ships were often stripped of weapons, charts, instruments, flags, tools, sailcloth, ropes, food and drink.

▲ VIKING HOARD

A hoard of Viking treasure reflects the wide area over which the warrior fleets raided and traded. It includes gold, silver and jewellery from the Anglo-Saxons and Franks of northern Europe. There are treasures, too, from the markets of Byzantium (modern Istanbul) and Baghdad. This hoard was buried at Hon in Norway in the AD860s to keep it safe from thieves.

◄ INCA GOLD

Solid gold figures were among treasures seized by Spanish invaders in the 1500s. The Spanish conquered many lands in Central and South America. They stripped the temples and palaces of the mighty Inca and Aztec empires of their gold. The native people were put to work in the silver mines of the Andes mountains. Soon mule trains were carrying untold riches to the Caribbean ports. The treasure ships that took the plunder to Spain were a prime target for pirates.

BARBARY PLUNDER ▶

The Barbary corsairs often robbed treasure ships, even though their chief aim was to seize Christians as slaves. Many ships sailing from Venice, Genoa and Spain were laden with precious cargoes. In those days, money and treasure was transported in chests from one country to another – there were no simple bank transfers as there are today.

▲ FACT OR FICTION?

Did pirates really bury their treasure, as shown in this illustration from the 1700s? There have always been rumours and local tales of hidden plunder. Some pirates may have hidden their ill-gotten gains, never to return. However, little pirate treasure has ever been found. What has been discovered is treasure hidden *from* pirates – by nervous monks or merchants expecting a raid. Pirates usually sold on their treasure. Objects from temples and churches were often melted down into gold or silver bars first.

▲ SURGEON'S CHEST

Medical supplies may not be our idea of treasure, but to pirates they were very precious indeed. They could make the difference between life and death. In 1718 Blackbeard threatened to murder hostages and set the North American port of Charleston ablaze if a valuable medicine chest was not sent out to his ship at once. As usual, his demands were met.

◀ TREASURE TROVE

In 1927, a hoard of gold and silver was discovered in the Church of San José in Panama. Had the treasure been hidden by anxious priests or townsfolk, or was the church used during looting by buccaneers? The treasure was believed to date from 1671, when the city was sacked by the Welsh pirate Henry Morgan. It took 175 mules to carry the gold and silver coins, jewellery, precious gemstones, silks and spices they had ransomed from their prisoners.

▲ EQUAL SHARES

A democratic pirate crew shares out the spoils. By the 1720s, the readiness of pirates to cheat and trick each other had become such a problem that rules were drawn up and agreed before a voyage began. Captain George Lowther's pirates agreed to split the loot into shares, with each crew member receiving one share, the captain two shares, the ship's master 1½ shares and the doctor, first mate, gunner and boatswain 1¼ shares each.

A Dead Man's Chest

Fifteen men on the dead man's chest –
Yo-ho-ho, and a bottle of rum!
Drink and the devil have done for the rest....

The song is from the classic pirate story *Treasure Island* written by Robert Louis Stevenson in 1881. Both song and book conjured up the image of pirates burying chests of treasure and drawing up secret maps. In reality this rarely happened. However, sea chests were used as early as Viking times for carrying a sailor's personal possessions and weapons. The strongest chests, fitted with iron bands and locks, were used to store gold, silver and other treasure on board ship.

> **You will need:** *50x 50cm corrugated cardboard, ruler, pencil, scissors, masking tape, cup of flour, about ½ cup of water, mixing bowl, fork, newspaper, fine sandpaper, brown acrylic paint, 5cm paintbrush, 25cm² black paper, white pencil, glue, matte wood varnish, 15 x 3cm black fabric.*
> **Pieces of eight:** *self-hardening clay, cocktail stick or meat skewer, gold and silver paints.*

When William Kidd returned to North America in 1699, he was said to be carrying £400,000-worth of plunder. He soon realized that he was going to be arrested for piracy, so he deposited shares of this treasure with friends. Eleven bags of silver and gold were left on Gardiner's Island, off Long Island, New York. The hoard was handed in to the authorities before Kidd's trial. There may be more still to be discovered. Teams have searched in Canada, others in Florida and the Caribbean – but none has ever been found.

1 Copy the templates on to the cardboard, carefully following the measurements shown above. Cut them out.

4 Place the flour in a bowl, and add water gradually, a spoon at a time. Mix as you go, to make a smooth, thick paste rather like pancake batter.

5 Tear the newspaper into strips and coat each strip with the paste. Cover the chest and lid, inside and out, with three layers of these strips.

9 Glue on the corner reinforcements. Glue the bands on the sides and bottom of the chest. Space them evenly and match them up with each other.

10 Glue the bands on the lid. Make sure you match up and continue the patterns that are on the sides and base of the chest. Varnish the chest and lid.

PIECES OF EIGHT

1 Mould the clay into ball shapes in the palms of your hands. Squash the balls into flat circles.

2 Look at real coins, or pictures of old coins. Engrave your coin designs with the cocktail stick.

3 Leave to harden and dry completely in a warm place. Then paint the coins gold and silver.

2 Use the masking tape to join the side sections **A** and **C** to each other and to the base **B** to make a box shape. Tape along the inside joins as well.

3 Tape together the lid sides **E** and **F** (there are two of each). Bend the top **D** to fit the curve of the lid and tape in place. Tape along all the inside joins of the lid.

6 Leave for several hours in a warm, dry place. When the surfaces are completely hard and dry, rub them down with fine sandpaper until smooth.

7 Paint the chest and lid, inside and out, with one or two coats of brown acrylic paint. Leave the first coat to dry before you apply the second coat.

8 Use the white pencil to draw the iron bands and corners on the black paper. Use a ruler to measure the strips to the same size as the chest. Cut them out.

You could line your chest with velvet to use as a money box or for your personal treasures. Pirate money would have been real gold and silver, such as the Spanish gold escudos (or doubloons) and the silver pesos of 8 reales (pieces-of-eight).

11 Take the black fabric strip and glue one half of it on to the inside back edge of the lid. It should be about half way along the lid edge.

12 Line up the lid and chest. Glue the other half of the fabric strip on to the inside back edge of the lower part of the chest to make a hinge.

Piratical Punishments

Some pirates carried out sickening acts of cruelty against their victims and may even have enjoyed doing so. Torture, burning and mutilation were common. Chinese pirates kept their captives in cramped bamboo cages, or nailed them to the deck. Such atrocities were more than mere punishments. They might be a quick way of extracting information about where gold was hidden, and they were certainly useful for spreading terror among future victims. Life at sea was tough, even on official naval ships. Any pirate who disobeyed ship's rules or quarrelled with his shipmates faced flogging, beating or being set adrift in a small boat. If a pirate robbed another member of the crew, he might be punished by having his ears and nose slit. The crew of John Phillips, captain of the *Revenge* around 1720, had to swear (over an axe rather than a Bible) that deserters and traitors would be marooned. This involved being set ashore and abandoned on a remote island with one flask of gunpowder, a pistol, ammunition and just one bottle of water – enough to last no more than a day or two.

▲ HOMESPUN PUNISHMENT

A person about to be punished had to make a cat o' nine tails before being flogged with it. Rope was unwound and knotted at the ends. The cat may have been used by pirates to give captured officers a taste of their own medicine.

◄ REVENGE

Pirates seize the arm of a ship's captain and hack it off. Many pirates who had served their time on merchant ships or in the Navy had bitter memories of ill treatment by officers. When they captured ships, they often sought revenge on the officers by torturing them.

TOO KIND BY HALF ►

The Irish pirate captain Edward England was punished by his crew for being too kindhearted. England's pirates were a constant threat to the great trading vessels of the East India Company. He is pictured here in front of the *Cassandra*, a ship he seized in the Comoro Islands in 1720. England gave the crew of the *Cassandra* the badly damaged pirate ship in exchange. The pirate crew was so furious at this act of mercy that they set England and his supporters adrift in a small boat. The men just managed to row across the Mozambique Channel to the island of Madagascar, where England soon died in poverty.

HUMAN SHOT ▶

French citizens of Algiers become ammunition in this gruesome illustration. Algiers was a corsair stronghold on the Barbary coast. European warships blockaded the port several times during the 1800s. In revenge, the Muslim defenders are said to have fired living French people at the enemy ships. Over the centuries, terrible tales were told of Barbary cruelty. Many of them were probably exaggerated. Even so, both sides did torture and abuse their prisoners and slaves.

▲ **ROASTED ALIVE**

An English sea captain is tortured over burning coals in India. Piracy was common along India's west coast to the south of Bombay. This scene may be meant to show Khanhoji Angria or his sons in the 1700s. These pirates from the Maratha states fought a bitter war against European shipping, demanding the right to control the region's trade. Their claim was fair, but they were dismissed as common pirates.

UNSTEADY WALK ▶

Pirates of the 1700s force a captive to walk the plank and fall into the sea, to drown or be eaten by sharks. Pirates did sometimes throw their victims overboard, but walking the plank seems to have been rare. The only known report of it happening is from a newspaper dated 1829.

Pirate Havens

Pirates have always needed bases, places where they could safely take on supplies and plan their next voyage. These havens needed to be easily defended and beyond the reach of the law. In the 1720s, the Welsh pirate captain Bartholomew Roberts and his crew holed up at a pirate colony in Sierra Leone, West Africa. It was run by a buccaneer called John Leadstone, or Old Crackers.

Sometimes pirates formed their own states, like miniature countries. On the shores of the Mediterranean Sea, there were entire colonies, founded by Greeks after about 700BC, that lived by piracy. Pirates who settled on the island of Madgascar off the East African coast about 300 years ago appointed themselves kings of the lands they seized.

The port of St Malo, in Brittany (in north-west France), lived by the corsair trade for hundreds of years. In the 1630s, the island of Tortuga, off Hispaniola in the Caribbean, was the chief base of the Caribbean buccaneers. Port Royal in Jamaica was another glory hole for pirates from the 1660s to the 1680s. It was followed a few years later by Nassau, in the Bahamas.

▲ A PROMISED LAND?

A pictorial map shows the luxuriant setting of a pirate stronghold on the African island of Madagascar. From the 1690s to the 1720s, thousands of pirates from Europe and the Americas settled here. It was said to be warm all the time, to have beautiful women and plentiful food. The island paradise was shortlived though, for naval patrols were soon rounding the Cape of Good Hope in pursuit of the pirates.

▲ SAFE HARBOUR

Lower the mainsail, cast the anchor! A battle-weary pirate crew sails into harbour to rest and re-stock. The place is perfect, with a cove hidden by craggy cliffs and a narrow entrance difficult for unwanted visitors to navigate. The hills are rich in vegetation. There will be lots of fresh fruit to pick, and wild animals and birds to hunt.

CITY OF THE CORSAIRS ▼

In 1762, an English fleet attacked the port of St Malo on the north coast of France, tired of falling prey to privateers. The people of St Malo made fortunes by encouraging privateering and demanding payment from English and Dutch shipping as it headed up the English Channel. The most famous privateer was René Du Guay-Trouin (1673-1736), who became a French naval commander.

◄ DRINK AND THE DEVIL

A pirate crew unwinds after several months at sea. Pirates were known for drinking too much alcohol such as wine, rum, gin and ale. They gambled too, playing at dice and cards, or placing bets on cockfights – to the death. Folk dances on the Atlantic coast of Nicaragua are said to have first been brought to the region by English pirates.

PIRATE KINGDOMS ►

It was easy for pirates to lord it over local people who lived on the island of Madagascar in the 1600s. Some of the pirates set up their own kingdoms. One of them was Abraham Samuel, a Jamaican of mixed descent. He ruled a patch of land in the south of the island at Fort Dauphin (modern Tôlanaro) in the 1690s. Another settlement was the self-styled kingdom of the pirate James Plantain, in the north of the island. Plantain called himself the King of Ranter Bay.

◄ JAMAICA RETREAT

A peaceful view of Port Royal, Jamaica, gives little idea of the port's rowdy taverns and slave markets. The British captured Jamaica from the Spanish in 1655. At first, buccaneers were allowed to use the port – provided they continued to attack Spanish ships. However, by the 1690s the colonial governors had had enough and set about eliminating the pirate menace. Port Royal (near modern-day Kingston), was destroyed by an earthquake in 1692.

Brought to Justice

In about 470BC, magistrates in the Greek city of Teos had to declare three times a year that anyone found guilty of piracy, plunder or trading with pirates would be killed, along with their families. In Roman times, pirates were nailed to wooden crosses and left to die. Between AD1000 and 1500, in the German port of Hamburg, hundreds of pirates were beheaded by sword. In the 1600s and 1700s, the bodies of hanged pirates were left in chains where they could be easily seen, on the sandy shores of Jamaica and the mudflats of the River Thames, as a warning to all.

In the end, it was modern technology rather than fear of punishment that brought most pirates to justice. Fast steamships, powerful guns and, eventually, radio communication left pirates with nowhere to hide. By the 1930s, piracy had become very rare.

Then, in the 1980s, piracy made a comeback, often under the new name of hijacking. Luxury yachts were attacked in the Caribbean and off Greece. In south-east Asia, large oil tankers were boarded by robbers armed with modern guns. The new pirates now had radio, firepower and fast boats. The details were different, but it was an ancient story.

▲ AWAITING THEIR FATE
No mercy is given and none is expected by pirates on trial. In the 1700s, new courts were set up to try pirates in Britain's American colonies. Naval officers and colonial governors passed judgment. Punishment was swift and merciless.

DEATH IN LONDON ▶
The body of a pirate is dragged through the streets, to be hacked apart and publicly burned. William de Marisco (or Marsh) was based on Lundy Island in the Bristol Channel off south-west England. He attacked ships all along the west coast until 1242, when he was captured, imprisoned in the Tower of London and then hanged.

END OF A PIRATE SQUADRON ▶
A Chinese pirate fleet was destroyed at Bias Bay, near Hong Kong, in September 1849. It was bombarded by a British naval force, and 400 pirates were killed. Pirate junks were destroyed on shore and piles of weapons were captured. The pirate chief, Cui A-Bao escaped justice, but only for a year or two. British efforts to stamp out piracy during the 1840s resulted in the deaths of over 2,000 pirates.

HANGED BY THE NECK ▶

Major Stede Bonnet, a plantation owner turned pirate, is hanged at Charleston, North America. He died on November 1718, together with 28 of his young crew. Bonnet had sailed with Blackbeard – and been cheated by him. He then operated along the coast of Virginia until he was caught. Colonial authorities in the Americas began clamping down on piracy in North American and Caribbean waters at the end of the 1600s. They placed bounties on pirates' heads as an incentive to capture them.

▲ THE DEATH MASK

A Chang Jiang River pirate gains immortality in this model cast from his head. Hundreds of Chinese pirates were beheaded in the 1800s. The executions were ordered by the Chinese Government and the European powers who governed some Chinese towns at that time. It was a brutal punishment, but one that the pirates had often practised on their own victims.

END OF AN AGE ▶

A group of Chinese pirates is beheaded at Kowloon in 1891. The last major period of piracy, based around the China Sea, was drawing to an end. Many of the pirates at that time were political rebels against both the Chinese Government and the foreign powers.

Timeline

There have been pirates as long as there have been trading ships to rob. The great age of piracy was during the 1600s and 1700s. It was a time when adventurers and explorers from Europe stormed their way around the world, greedy for treasure and power. Piracy became less common after the 1800s, but does still take place today.

700–100BC

565 GREEKS settle on the island of Corsica in the Mediterranean Sea and live by piracy.

532 POLYKRATES comes to power on the Greek island of Samos and turns to piracy, robbing friend and foe alike.

330 ALEXANDER THE GREAT tries to put an end to piracy in the Mediterranean – without a great deal of success.

Alexander the Great

Alexander the Great tackles Greek pirates

99BC–AD699

60sBC THE ROMAN EMPEROR POMPEY launches a 3-month campaign to end Mediterranean piracy. Ten thousand pirates are killed.

350s SHAPUR, RULER OF PERSIA tries to rid the Persian Gulf of pirates.

450s PRINCESS ALWILDA OF GOTLAND terrorizes the coast of the Baltic Sea.

450s IRISH PIRATES raid western British Isles.

Princess Alwilda

1500–1520s

1504 BARBARY CORSAIRS, under the Barbarossa brothers, capture papal treasure galleys in the Mediterranean.

1511 SCOTTISH PRIVATEER Andrew Barton plunders shipping off the coast of Flanders.

1522 GENOESE SEA CAPTAIN VERRAZANO, in French service, attacks a Spanish treasure fleet returning from the New World.

1523 ATTACK ON A SPANISH TREASURE FLEET returning from the New World, by French privateer Jean Fleury off Portugal.

Barbarossa brothers

1530–1550s

1545 ROBERT RENEGER, seafarer from Southampton, England, captures the Spanish treasure galleon San Salvador off Portugal.

1553 FRENCH PRIVATEER, FRANÇOIS LE CLERC, often known as Jambe de Bois (wooden leg) attacks the Spanish.

1553 THE TURKISH CORSAIRS Dragut and Sinan occupy Tripoli (Libya).

1558 THOMAS STUCLEY, a noble-born rogue from Devon, England, is accused of piracy.

Spanish treasure ships attacked

1560s

1560-85 GRAINNE NI MHAILLE (GRACE O'MALLEY) runs a pirate fleet on Ireland's Atlantic coast.

1562 ENGLISH PRIVATEER JOHN HAWKINS starts trading slaves between West Africa and the Caribbean.

1568–72 CHANNEL PRIVATEERING by English, French and Dutch reaches its peak.

1569 DUTCH PRIVATEERS called the Sea Beggars start a campaign against Spanish ships and troops in the Netherlands.

Privateering in the English Channel

1660s & 70s

1660s BUCCANEERS attack Spanish treasure fleets in the Caribbean. Maltese corsairs attack Muslim fleets in the Mediterranean.

1668 WELSH PIRATE HENRY MORGAN leads buccaneer army into Puerto del Principe, on Spanish Cuba.

1674 HENRY MORGAN becomes the Lieutenant Governor of Jamaica.

1678 ALEXANDRE EXQUEMELIN, French surgeon and buccaneer, writes *Bucaniers of America*.

Jamaican rum

1680s

1680 BUCCANEER BARTHOLOMEW SHARP leads a plundering voyage around South America.

1681 LANCELOT BLACKBURNE, an English priest, keeps company with the Caribbean buccaneers. He later becomes Archbishop of York.

1688 HENRY MORGAN dies of drink.

1689 WILLIAM KIDD first serves as a privateer captain, in the Caribbean.

1689 MADAGASCAR becomes pirate haven, under pirate King Abraham Samuel.

Feasting in Madagascar

1690s

1690 THE PIRATE ROUND – from the Americas to the Indian Ocean via Africa – is established.

1692 PORT ROYAL, Jamaica, favourite haunt of buccaneers and pirates, is destroyed by an earthquake.

1693 AMERICAN PIRATE THOMAS TEW leaves Bermuda for the Indian Ocean.

1694 JEAN BART, a corsair from Dunkirk, is captured by the English – and escapes.

John Bart

1730–99

1736 DEATH OF FRENCH PRIVATEER René Duguay-Trouin, a St Malo corsair.

1756 FINAL DEFEAT of Maratha pirates in India.

1779 AMERICAN COLONIAL PRIVATEERS, such as Paul Jones, attack British shipping.

1795 FRENCH PRIVATEER ROBERT SURCOUF of St Malo attacks British shipping in the Indian Ocean.

Indian pirate torture

1800-1810

1803 AMERICAN FLEET makes an attack on Barbary pirates.

1807-10 QING ER SOU (MADAM CHENG) takes control of a vast pirate fleet in the South China Sea following her husband's death.

1809 BRITISH FLEET DESTROYS PIRATE BASE at Ras al Khaima in the Persian Gulf.

1810 FRENCH PIRATE JEAN LAFITTE attacks ships sailing out of New Orleans in the southern states of North America.

Qing Er Sou leads attack

1810s

1812 JEAN LAFITTE becomes an official privateer in the service of America.

1816 ANGLO-DUTCH FLEET bombards Algiers to oust Barbary corsairs.

1819 ANTI-PIRACY TASK FORCE destroys pirate bases in the Persian Gulf.

Prisoners shot from Barbary mortars

AD 700–1010

789 VIKING PIRATES begin to raid coastal settlements in the British Isles.

846 VIKING LEADER RAGNAR LODBROK besieges Paris.

859 VIKING WARRIOR BJORN IRONSIDE sails for the Mediterranean in search of plunder.

860-914 VIKINGS threaten Constantinople (modern Istanbul).

885 A VIKING ARMY attacks the city of Paris.

1009 VIKING OLAF THE STOUT pulls down London Bridge.

Olaf the Stout

1200s

1217 FLEMISH-BORN EUSTACE THE BLACK MONK is beheaded in a sea battle off Sandwich, England.

1242 WILLIAM DE MARISCO (MARSH) of Lundy Island is captured, hanged, quartered and burned in London.

1243 EARLY EXAMPLE OF LETTER OF MARQUE is issued by King Henry III of England.

1281 KUBLAI KHAN, Mongol emperor of China, launches unsuccessful attacks on Japan in response to Japanese piracy.

William de Marisco

1300–1499

1394 HARRY PAY, sailing out of Poole, England, sacks the Spanish port of Gijon.

1399 PRIVATEER JOHN HAWLEY of Dartmouth, England, captures 34 vessels sailing from Normandy and Brittany.

1402 STÖRTEBEKER leader of the Baltic pirate band, the Friends of God and Enemies of the World, is executed in Germany.

1406 HARRY PAY escapes the French and attacks ships in the River Seine.

1492 FIRST VOYAGE of Christopher Columbus, in the service of Spain, across Atlantic to the W Indies.

Spanish treasure

1570s & 80s

1572 ENGLISH SEAFARER FRANCIS DRAKE attacks Spanish at Nombre de Dios, a port on the Isthmus of Panama.

1573 THIRTY-THREE GERMAN PIRATES AND THEIR LEADER KLEIN HENSZLEIN are executed in Hamburg, Germany.

1578 FRANCIS DRAKE raids Spain's Pacific ports.

1580 JOHN OXENHAM, DRAKE'S LIEUTENANT, is captured by the Spanish and hanged for piracy.

1582 LADY MARY KILLIGREW leads Cornish pirates against a Spanish ship that is taking refuge from storms in Falmouth.

1586 FRANCIS DRAKE attacks Spanish at Cartagena in Colombia, South America.

1600s & 1610s

1601 USKOK PIRATES from Segna, near Fiume (modern Rijeka in Croatia), attack Venetian shipping.

1607 ENGLISH NOBLEMAN SIR FRANCIS VERNEY joins the Muslim Barbary corsairs.

1611 DUTCH PIRATE SIMON DANZIGER, also known as Captain Devil, is hanged at Tunis, North Africa, after becoming a Barbary corsair and then rejoining the Christians.

1612 THE ENGLISH PIRATE PETER EASTON leads a large pirate fleet to the Mediterranean to plunder merchant shipping.

Mediterranian corsair

1620s–50s

1620 PIRATE REPUBLIC is declared at Sallee, a territory on the Atlantic coast of Morocco.

1627 DUTCH PRIVATEER JAN JANSZ joins the Barbary corsairs and leads a slave raid on Iceland.

1630 THE ISLAND OF TORTUGA in the Caribbean becomes a buccaneer base.

1642 CAPTAIN WILLIAM JACKSON, English privateer, signs up 1,000 men to plunder the Spanish Main.

1650 MAJOR SPANISH OFFENSIVE against camps of British buccaneers.

1700–1709

1700 THE FIRST RECORD OF A BLACK JACK with skull-and-crossbones being flown.

Calico Jack's black jack flag

1701 CAPTAIN KIDD hanged in London for piracy.

1705 THOMAS GREEN, pirate captain, and 16 of his crew hanged in Edinburgh, Scotland.

Blackbeard

1710s

1716-18 NEW PROVIDENCE BAHAMAS, is established as a major pirate base.

1717 THE PIRATE SHIP WHYDAH, commanded by Sam Bellamy, is wrecked on the coast of Cape Cod, America.

1718 MAJOR STEDE BONNET, plantation owner turned pirate, is hanged. EDWARD TEACH (Blackbeard) is killed.

1718 CHRISTOPHER CONDENT attacks shipping off Africa and Arabia.

1719 HOWELL DAVIS, Welsh pirate, dies on Africa's Guinea Coast. BARTHOLOMEW ROBERTS, Welsh pirate, leads devastating attacks on Guinea coast.

1720s

1720 MARY READ AND ANNE BONNY are brought to trial in Jamaica. Their associate, CALICO JACK RACKHAM, is hanged. PIRATE CHARLES VANE is hanged in Jamaica.

1720s PIRATE JAMES PLANTAIN declares himself king of Ranter Bay, Madagasar.

1722 BARTHOLOMEW ROBERTS' pirate crew captured in Africa, 52 hanged. MATHEW LUKE's pirate crew tried in Jamaica, 41 hanged.

1723 THOMAS ANSTIS Pirate captain is murdered in Caribbean by his own crew.

Mary Read

1820s–40s

1826 RAHMAH BIN JABR, an Arab pirate, aged 70, blows up his own ship in battle.

1827 BENITO DE SOTO, a Spanish pirate, attacks Atlantic shipping.

1843 BRITISH BEGIN CAMPAIGN against Dayak pirate bases in Borneo and Sulu Sea.

1849 BRITISH DESTROY CHINESE PIRATE fleet off the Vietnam coast.

Chinese pirate beheads his victim

1850s–60s

1851 CUI A-BAO, lieutenant of CHINESE PIRATE CHIEF SHI WU-ZAI, kills himself in jail.

1843 BRITISH BEGIN CAMPAIGN against Dayak pirate bases in Borneo and Sulu Sea.

1849 BRITISH DESTROY THE LAST CHINESE PIRATE fleet off the coast of Vietnam.

1856 PRIVATEERING ABOLISHED by Britain, France and Russia.

1857 ELI BOGGS, an American pirate, is captured in the South China Sea by American merchant captain and rogue Henry Hayes.

pirate junk

1900s

airline hijacked

oil tanker attacked

a1920s–30s LAST DAYS OF CHINESE PIRACY as political rebels take to the sea.

1985 *ACHILLE LAURO*, an Italian cruise liner is hijacked by Palestinian terrorists.

1992 THE BRITISH NAVY in South-east Asia launches piracy patrol after supertanker is attacked by pirates.

GLOSSARY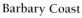

Barbary Coast
A section of the North African coast famed for its corsairs (from Berbers, the people of the region).

becalmed
The state of a sailing ship when it cannot move because there is no wind.

bilge
The lowest section of a ship's hull.

blackjack
A black pirate flag.

boom
The spar to which a sail is attached so that it can be moved according to wind direction.

bow
The front, pointed part of a ship.

bowsprit
A long spar projecting from a ship's prow.

brigantine
A two-masted sailing ship, square-rigged on both masts, with a fore-and-aft sail on the lower part of the mainmast.

buccaneers
Pirates and privateers who plundered Spanish ships and treasure ports in the West Indies and Central America in the 1600s.

calico
A type of cotton cloth, either white or boldly patterned.

capstan
Winding gear, used for raising anchors or sails.

careen
To beach a ship, so its hull can be cleaned and repaired.

caulk
To seal leaking ship's timbers with fibre and pitch (tar).

corsair
(1) A pirate or a privateer, especially in the Mediterranean region and northern France.
(2) The ship sailed by (1).

crow's nest
A small platform high up on a mast, which is used as a lookout position.

cutlass
A slashing sword used by sailors from the 1600s onwards.

dhow
An Arab sailing ship with one or two masts and triangular sails.

draught
The depth of the ship below water, which is also the maximum depth of water it can float in.

East Indiaman
A large English or Dutch merchant vessel that traded with Asia.

ensign
A flag flown from the stern of a ship.

figurehead
A decorative wooden figure found on the prow of some sailing ships.

filibuster
A French buccaneer.

flintlock pistol
An early type of pistol in which a piece of flint is made to spark and set off the gunpowder.

fo'c'sle
An abbreviation of forecastle, the raised deck at the front of a ship.

fore-and-aft
Having sails that are lined up with the length of the ship (the opposite of square-rigged).

furl
Gathering in and folding up a sail.

fuse
A slow-burning length of cord that is used to set off the charge in a cannon.

galleon
A big sailing ship with three or more masts, used from the 1500s to the 1700s as a warship and a Spanish treasure ship.

galley
(1) Any large ship powered by oars.
(2) A ship's kitchen.

grappling iron
Metal hooks attached to a long rope. They were thrown on to an enemy ship to help boarding.

Guinea Coast
The coast around the Gulf of Guinea (West Africa).

gunport
An opening in a ship's side through which a cannon was fired.

halyard
A rope used to hoist a flag or a sail.

hard tack
Ship's biscuits.

hourglass
A primitive instrument for telling the time, which uses sand running through a glass tube to indicate the passing of one hour.

hull
The main, outer body of a ship.

jack
A square flag flown from the front of a ship indicating nationality.

jib
A triangular sail that is set at the front of a ship between the foremast and bowsprit.

Jolly Roger
The common term for any pirate flag.

junk
(1) A wooden sailing ship commonly used in China and the Far East.
(2) Bits of old rope used for caulking.
(3) Salted meat.

landlubber
A person with little experience of life at sea.

letter of marque
A licence or certificate issued by a monarch or government, authorizing the bearer to attack enemy shipping.

log-book
A written record of a ship's voyage, noting course, speed and daily events.

longship
A long, streamlined wooden ship sailed by Viking raiders and explorers.

magazine
The place where gunpowder is stored on a ship.

Malouin
A person from the port of St Malo, in France.

marlinspike
A metal spike used to separate strands of rope.

maroon
To set someone ashore on a remote island, to abandon.

mizzen
The rear sail on a three-masted vessel.

musket
An early type of gun.

mutiny
To refuse to obey an officer's orders, or open revolt on board ship.

oakum
Old rope fibres, unpicked and used for caulking.

pennant
A triangular flag or streamer flown from a mast-top.

pieces of eight
Silver pesos (Spanish coins), which were worth eight reales.

piracy
Robbery at sea, stealing or destruction of ships, coastal raiding.

piragua
A small sailing canoe used by the early buccaneers in the Caribbean.

Pirate Round
A popular route taken by pirates from the 1690s onwards – North America or the Caribbean to West Africa, Madagascar, the Red Sea and then back across the Atlantic Ocean.

prahu
A type of wooden galley used in south-east Asia.

press
To force someone to join a ship's crew.

privateer
(1) Someone who is legally authorized to attack the ships of an enemy.
(2) The ship sailed by (1).

prow
The bow (front) of a ship.

ratlines
Cross-ropes on the shrouds, forming a rope ladder that enables the sailors to climb to the top of the mast.

renegade
Someone who changes sides, a turncoat or traitor.

sack
To raid or plunder, usually including robbery and destruction.

schooner
A small, fast sailing ship, which usually has two masts rigged fore-and-aft.

scurvy
A disease caused by a lack of Vitamin C in the diet. Symptoms include bleeding gums and spots.

sea-beggar
A member of a famous band of Dutch privateers.

shot
Ammunition of iron or lead that is fired from a musket or a cannon.

shrouds
Ropes running from the side of a ship to the top of its mast in order to support it.

sloop
A fast, small, single-masted sailing ship.

Spanish Main
(1) The Spanish-ruled mainland of Central and South America.
(2) The Caribbean region and the Gulf of Mexico.

spar
A wooden pole used for the mast or yard of a sailing vessel.

splice
To interweave two rope ends in order to join them.

spritsail
A sail hanging from a spar beneath the bowsprit.

square-rigged
Having square sails set at right angles to the mast (the opposite of fore-and-aft).

staff
(1) A pole on which a flag is hung.
(2) A length of wood marked with measurements used to calculate angles and distances in navigating.

stern
The back end of a ship.

topgallant
A sail above the topsail.

topsail
A sail above the mainsail or foresail.

yard
The spar (wooden pole) to which the top of a sail is attached.

INDEX 💀